C0-DAP-371

Water

Steck Vaughn™

HOUGHTON MIFFLIN HARCOURT
Supplemental Publishers

www.SteckVaughn.com
800-531-5015

Water

contents

Water
Fact Matters

ISBN-13: 978-1-4190-5475-4
ISBN-10: 1-4190-5475-9

First published by Blake Education Pty Ltd as *Go Facts*
Copyright © 2006 Blake Publishing
This edition copyright under license from Blake Education Pty Ltd
© 2010 Steck-Vaughn, an imprint of HMH Supplemental Publishers Inc.

All rights reserved. No part of the material protected by this copyright may be reproduced or utilized in any form or by any means, in whole or in part, without permission in writing from the Publisher. Requests for permission should be mailed to: Paralegal Department, 6277 Sea Harbor Drive, Orlando, FL 32887.

Steck-Vaughn is a trademark of HMH Supplemental Publishers Inc.

Printed in China

If you have received these materials as examination copies free of charge, HMH Supplemental Publishers Inc. retains title to the materials and they may not be resold. Resale of examination copies is strictly prohibited.

Possession of this publication in print format does not entitle users to convert this publication, or any portion of it, into electronic format.

1 2 3 4 5 6 7 8   373   15 14 13 12 11 10 09 08

The Rarest Kind of Water

About three-quarters of our planet is covered by water. Almost all of it is salt water. Fresh water doesn't contain salt. It is only about three percent of the water on Earth.

Essential Fresh Water

Fresh water is necessary for life. People and animals drink fresh water. Plants need water to grow. We use fresh water for our homes, **industry**, and **agriculture**.

Most of the world's fresh water is frozen in **glaciers**, **ice sheets**, and **ice caps**. Glaciers are slow-moving bodies of ice made from snow buildup. Ice caps are masses of ice that cover areas of land. Ice sheets are very large ice caps. There are **massive** ice sheets in Antarctica and Greenland.

On the Surface, Under the Ground

The rest of the world's fresh water is found in lakes and rivers and is called surface water. Fresh water located under the ground is called groundwater. Most of the water we use is the result of rain seeping into the ground. This is the **source** of wells and springs.

Conserving Water

The amount of water on our planet never changes. However, fresh water can become **polluted** and unusable by humans. Since the amount of fresh water we have is limited, we must conserve this resource and stop it from becoming polluted.

Did You Know?

The Antarctic ice sheet holds about 90 percent of the Earth's ice.

Groundwater includes water flowing between rocks and soil, moisture in the soil, frozen soil, and underground rivers.

Did You Know?

Australia is the driest inhabited continent. It has the lowest rainfall.

The Water Cycle

The movement of water between the land, the oceans, and the atmosphere is called the **water cycle***.*

Three Forms

Water can exist in three different forms: solid, liquid, and gas. The heat of the Sun changes liquid water into invisible water vapor, which is a gas. This process is called **evaporation**. Water also evaporates from the soil and from the leaves of plants. This is called transpiration.

Water Up and Down

Water vapor rises into the atmosphere. As the vapor rises, it gets colder and changes back into a liquid. It forms very small water droplets. This change is called **condensation**. The water droplets can freeze into solid ice or snow.

These droplets form clouds. The droplets grow too big and heavy to stay in the air. Then they fall back to Earth as rain, hail, mist, or snow. This is called **precipitation**.

Going Underground

Infiltration happens when water soaks into the soil. Water that flows across the ground and doesn't soak into the soil is called runoff. Some of the water will be soaked up by roots to help plants grow. The rest moves slowly between the soil and rocks as groundwater. Groundwater eventually flows to the surface again. It can also flow into the ocean. Groundwater is often brought to the surface by wells made by humans.

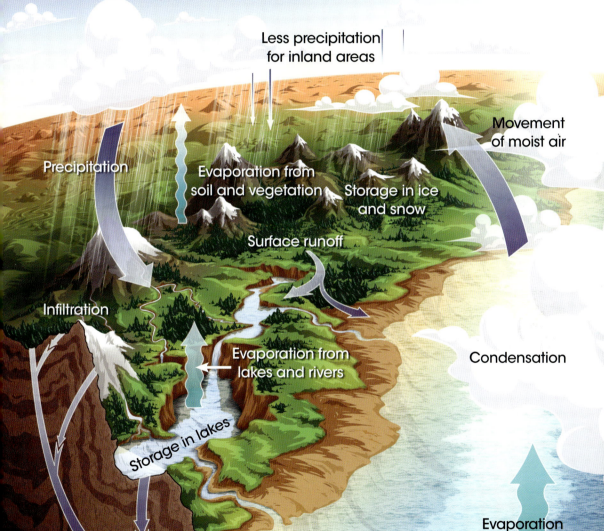

Did You Know?

Raindrops are not tear-shaped. Scientists have discovered that raindrops resemble the shape of a hamburger bun!

Less precipitation for inland areas

Movement of moist air

Precipitation

Evaporation from soil and vegetation

Storage in ice and snow

Surface runoff

Infiltration

Evaporation from lakes and rivers

Condensation

Storage in lakes

Evaporation from oceans

Groundwater flow

Storage in oceans

Finding Fresh Water

People access the fresh water stored in rivers, lakes, ice, and underground in different ways.

Stored Water

Most of the water we use comes from rivers, lakes, and **dams**.

A river starts from melting ice, rainfall, or a lake. It grows as streams in its catchment area join it.

Lakes can be natural or artificial. Artificial lakes are known as **reservoirs**. Reservoirs are made by building a dam across a river. The dam causes water to collect on one side. Water is then pumped from the dam through pipes to cities and towns. Farmers might pump water directly from rivers to use on their crops.

Digging for Water

Groundwater is an important source of fresh water. The water collects above a layer of rock that is too **dense** to allow it to flow through. People dig wells to access this water. Groundwater is the most **accessible** source of fresh water in the world. About 1.5 billion people use it for their drinking water.

Most of the frozen fresh water is located at the North and South Poles. But this is a long way from where most people live. Some glaciers partially melt in summer. This melted water forms rivers. Many people in China, India, Ecuador, Peru, and Bolivia get their fresh water this way.

Icebergs are blocks of frozen fresh water floating in saltwater oceans.

Did You Know?

Seven rivers in Asia are fed by glaciers in the Himalayas. These rivers supply water to hundreds of millions of people.

Water frozen in glaciers, ice caps, and ice sheets makes up 70 percent of the fresh water on Earth.

Water and Industry

Water is used for different purposes in many industries. Industries must be careful how they get rid of water they use to avoid damaging the environment.

How Industries Use Water

Most water supplied to industries comes from the same source as household water. Some industries use water for cooling and cleaning. Others use water as an ingredient in making food. Water is also used to **generate** electricity, to mix chemicals, and to wash away waste materials.

Factories need fresh water. Salt water can damage machines. The mining, steel, paper, and chemical industries use a lot of water.

Dealing with Waste Water

Industries must follow strict rules about safely getting rid of waste water. Modern factories have machines that use less water and cause less pollution than machines in earlier factories. In some factories, recycled water is piped back to the factory after it has been cleaned. Some factories recycle their water themselves. This keeps chemicals and industrial waste out of the freshwater supply and groundwater.

Water is an important part of the process of producing electricity at a nuclear power plant.

Some industries, such as the chemical industry, use and pollute large amounts of water.

Did You Know?

Water can generate **hydroelectric** power. Water is released from dams into turbines that spin to generate electricity. The water is then directed to a river or reservoir to be reused. Unlike burning coal, hydroelectric power doesn't produce gases that harm the Earth.

Water and Agriculture

*About 70 percent of the fresh water we use is for **irrigating** food crops and pastures.*

Surface, Sprinkler, and Drip Irrigation

There are different ways of irrigating land. Some use less water than others. The type of irrigation chosen depends on cost, availability of equipment, the type of soil, and the crop being grown.

In surface irrigation, the water moves across the ground through gravity. The most common type is furrow irrigation. Channels, or ditches, are dug in the land for water to run down. Furrow irrigation is usually used when crops are planted in a row.

In sprinkler irrigation, water

is piped to a central location. Sprinkler systems spray water onto a crop. Sprinklers wet the whole plant, not just the roots. This type of irrigation is similar to rain falling.

Drip irrigation is used in very hot climates or when there is a shortage of water. Pipes with very small openings are laid along the ground near the plants' roots. Water drips slowly out of the openings. This is an effective way to use less water. But it can only be used in small areas and for certain crops.

Flooding the Soil

Some crops, such as rice, grow best when flooded. The soil is prepared for planting, then water is allowed to flood onto it. The rice seedlings are planted and left to grow. The water is then drained from the field. The rice dries before it is harvested.

Furrow irrigation is being used here.

Producing:	uses this many liters of water:
one sheet of paper	10
one slice of bread	40
one egg	135
one cup of coffee	140
one glass of milk	200
one cotton t-shirt	2,000
one hamburger	2,400
one pair of shoes	8,000

A pivot sprinkler irrigates large circular fields.

Water Pollution

Water is polluted by industry, agriculture, and communities. Pollution makes water unfit to drink.

Sources of Pollution

The major causes of water pollution are chemicals, **pesticides**, **fertilizers**, untreated **sewage**, factory waste water, and litter from storm water drains.

When industries return water to the water supply, it can contain chemicals, oils, and other **pollutants**.

Too Much Algae

Farmers use chemical fertilizers and pesticides on their crops. When it rains, some of these chemicals may wash into rivers. This can cause algal bloom in lakes and rivers. Algal bloom is the rapid growth of algae on the water's surface. The algae block out sunlight and use up oxygen in the water. Fish and plants need oxygen to live. Algal bloom can kill them. Some algae are poisonous and make the water undrinkable.

Bad Rain

Heavily polluted air can mix with the water in clouds. The polluted water falls back to Earth as **acid rain**. Acid rain can make the soil so acidic that trees can't grow. Too much acid in lakes and rivers kills fish and frogs. This means the waterbird population won't have enough food.

Storm water drains carry rainwater away from cities and towns to dams, rivers, and oceans. But this runoff includes litter from the streets.

Each year plastic waste in water and coastal areas kills up to one million seabirds.

Polluted water greatly increases the risk of diseases such as hepatitis, cholera, dysentery, and typhoid.

Pesticides sprayed from a plane can easily drift into lakes and rivers.

More than four trillion cigarette butts are littered every year. Cigarette butts have been found in the stomachs of birds and sea turtles.

Water and Your Home

Many people in the world have access to lots of clean fresh water. How does it get to their homes?

Fresh water is pumped from a lake or dam to a water filtration plant. There it is filtered to remove weeds, fish, and minerals. It is then pumped into storage tanks.

From the storage tanks it moves into underground **water mains**. These carry water to taps in our houses. When we open a tap, the pressure in the pipes pushes the water out. Water pipes can also be connected directly to wells or boreholes to provide water to houses not connected to the water mains.

Using Less

In industrialized countries, each person uses up to 260 gallons of water every day to drink, cook, wash, flush toilets, and water gardens. But in countries where water is not piped into houses, people use as little as one gallon per day.

We cannot drink less water. But we can find other ways to use less water:

- Repair dripping taps.
- Take a quick shower instead of a bath.
- Wash dishes in a sink filled with water, not under a running tap.
- Wash the car with a bucket of water instead of a hose.
- Water the garden at cool times of the day.

What are other ways to conserve water?

Did You Know?

Waste water from washing machines, dishwashers, kitchen sinks, baths, and showers is called gray water. It can be used instead of fresh water to water the garden.

Cleaning Our Drinking Water

*Drinking water is water that is safe for humans. People can drink it and use it for cooking, washing, and bathing. Water is cleaned and **purified** before it is ready to drink.*

Sinking Sediment

Water is pumped from a river, lake, or dam into a tank. A chemical called alum is added to the water. This causes **impurities** in the water to thicken into small particles called flocs.

The water is then moved to a sedimentation tank. The flocs attract dirt and sink to the bottom as sediment. The clear water above the sediment is pumped to the next stage, which is filtration.

Removing Particles

The water is filtered through layers of sand, gravel, or charcoal. This is to remove the tiny particles that have not become sediment. This works in the same way that rocks and soil filter groundwater.

The filtered water is treated, often with chlorine, to kill bacteria and any harmful **microscopic** organisms. In some countries, fluoride is added to the water to help prevent tooth decay.

Water from the Sea

Salt water can be turned into drinking water by **desalination**. This process removes salt and other impurities from sea water. It is used in parts of the world, such as Israel, where fresh water is **scarce**.

One way to desalinate sea water is to force sea water through a membrane under high pressure. The membrane acts like a strainer. It stops salt from passing through. But it does allow fresh water to go through.

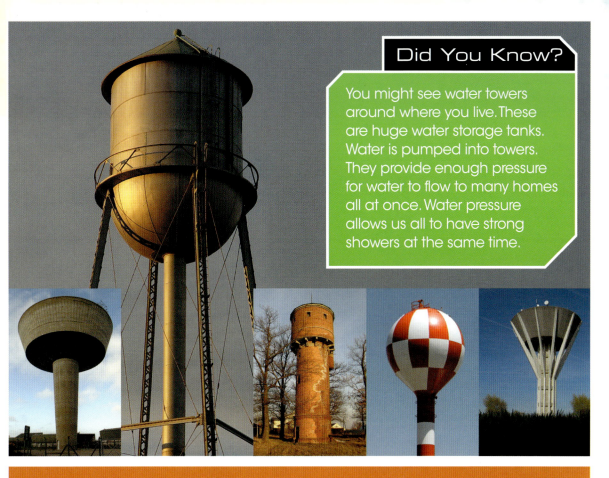

Did You Know?

You might see water towers around where you live. These are huge water storage tanks. Water is pumped into towers. They provide enough pressure for water to flow to many homes all at once. Water pressure allows us all to have strong showers at the same time.

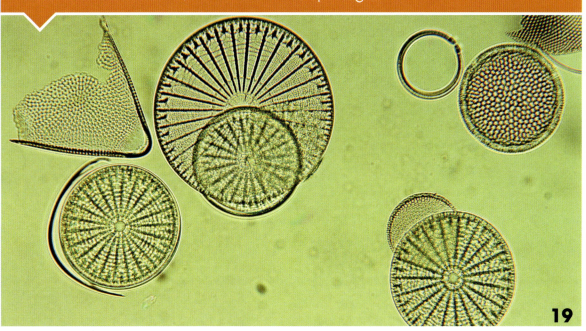

Even water that looks clean can contain things you wouldn't want to drink, like these microscopic algae.

Filter Your Own Water

You can make your own filter to clean water. Remember, filtered water must also be purified of germs or bacteria. Only then is it safe to drink.

You will need:

- two clear containers, such as soft drink bottles
- a funnel (see instructions to make one)
- coffee filter paper, a paper towel, or a piece of cloth
- gravel, dried beans, or crushed eggshells
- sand or uncooked rice
- dirty water (see recipe)

To make a funnel: Curl a piece of paper into a cone shape and tape it together. Make a tiny opening at the bottom for water to drip through.

To make dirty water: Fill one of your containers about halfway with water. Add a spoonful of sand, dust, bits of leaves, grass, or powdered soap. Shake it up.

You should see cleaner, clearer water after the following procedure. Repeat the process to see if the water gets clearer. **Do not drink the water!** It may still contain harmful germs and bacteria. You can use the water for plants.

1 Line the funnel with the coffee filter paper, a paper towel, or a cloth.

2 Make a layer of either sand or uncooked rice in the funnel.

3 Make another layer on top of this with gravel, dried beans, or crushed eggshells.

4 Hold the funnel over the empty container. Slowly pour the dirty water into the funnel and watch as it drips through the filter.

Wetlands

*A **wetland** is exactly what the name suggests. It's wet land. Wetlands help keep the freshwater supply clean. They also protect the land from floods.*

Types of Wetlands

Wetlands aren't wet all year round. But they are wet for long periods. They typically contain shallow water that is fresh water, salt water, or a mix of the two, called **brackish** water. Marshes, mangroves, swamps, bogs, and fens are all wetlands.

Wetlands act as natural water filters. Their soil is like a sponge, holding large amounts of water. When there is heavy rain, wetlands absorb the water. They release it slowly later. This helps prevent flooding of the surrounding land.

Dangerous Wetlands?

Wetlands were once seen as damp, dangerous places that caused diseases. They were used as dumping grounds for trash and sewage. Many wetlands were destroyed to create more land for agriculture and building.

Heavy rain then went straight into rivers rather than wetlands, and it contributed to flooding. Wetlands are breeding grounds for fish and other aquatic life. Their loss damaged fishing industries.

The United States has lost 53 percent of its wetlands. California alone has lost 91 percent of its wetlands.

Wetlands, like these in Florida, occur in every country. Wetlands cover roughly six percent of the Earth's land surface.

Mangrove wetlands are an important breeding ground for fish and birds.

These volunteers are collecting trash and cleaning up the land.

The Everglades

The Everglades is a large wetland in southern Florida. It was once a clean wetlands system, but people damaged the natural habitat by changing the flow of water.

Wet Summer, Dry Winter

Water in the Everglades flowed and dried up in a natural cycle. After summer rains, the Everglades flowed steadily to the ocean. The water in the Everglades was about 50 miles wide but less than a foot deep. The area was known as "the river of grass."

After the rains there would be six months of dry weather. Alligators built their nests above the water level. Migrating waterbirds ate the plants that had been underwater in summer. They also ate the fish that had moved into shallower pools.

Shrinking Wetland

People needed more land. Canals were built to control floods. The water in the Everglades was drained for agriculture and drinking water and shrank to half its original size. The regular flow of water stopped. The water became polluted by fertilizers and pesticides. Sometimes water was released into the Everglades in winter. This flooded the dry areas in the wrong season, destroying alligator nests and scattering the food of migrating birds.

Redirecting the Water

The people of Florida realized that they needed a healthy Everglades for a healthy environment. Since 1993 water flow has been increased. Marsh filtering systems have been built to clean the water. In the future more fresh water will be sent to the parts of the Everglades that need it most.

The river of grass still supplies water to major cities, such as Miami.

The Everglades National Park is the only place in the world where alligators and crocodiles exist side by side.

The great blue heron and the Florida panther make their home in the Everglades.

Dams

A dam is a barrier built to stop the flow of water. Dams have been built since ancient times. They allow people to store water. They prevent rivers from flooding. But building dams can also harm **ecosystems** *and people's lives.*

Benefits

Early, simple dams were built with soil and branches. They blocked water flow in a stream. Reservoirs were dug alongside the stream or river. Channels were then built to direct the water into the reservoirs. Water was pumped or carried to homes and farmlands.

Modern dams are enormous. They control flooding and provide a dependable supply of drinking water. The water can also be used to irrigate crops and generate hydroelectricity. People also use dams and reservoirs for recreation, such as boating and waterskiing.

Problems

A large dam is expensive. It takes many years to build. Dams flood a lot of land that could be used for housing or agriculture. Some people have to move because the land they live on will become flooded.

Dams also have negative effects on the environment. They can disrupt ecosystems in and around rivers. They can stop the natural flow of water into wetlands.

The Aswan High Dam in Egypt was built to prevent the Nile River from flooding. It also generates electricity and provides water for agriculture. It has created a huge reservoir behind the dam wall.

Reservoir

Dam

Nile River

Fort Peck Dam in Montana releases about 6.5 billion gallons of water a day!

Did You Know?

The Three Gorges Dam in China will be complete in 2011. It will control floods farther down the Yangtze River.

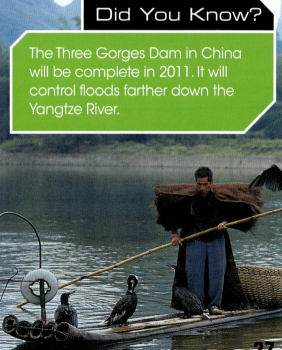

Water for Everyone?

All humans need water to survive. In modern industrialized countries, clean water is easy to find. We simply turn on a tap. But more than one billion people in the world do not have access to clean, safe water.

Not Enough Water

In unindustrialized countries, many people cannot get enough water for drinking and cooking. If they can find water, they may have to carry it long distances from rivers and wells. Children spend a large part of every day fetching water. This prevents them from being able to go to school.

Dirty Water Danger

People don't have flushing toilets and sewage systems if there is not running water. Human and animal waste ends up in rivers. This can cause diseases. Millions of people die every year from diseases related to water pollution.

The United Nations (UN) has created the Millennium Development Goals in an attempt to improve the quality of life for people everywhere. The UN wants the number of people who don't have sustainable access to safe drinking water and basic **sanitation** to be halved by the year 2015. This big goal can be achieved. But governments must be willing to provide enough money for water and sanitation for the world's poorest people.

A protected well and pump provide clean water to students of Shambarai Primary School in Tanzania.

This well in Mali isn't deep enough to reach a steady supply of water.

Over one billion people in the world do not have access to unpolluted water.

A capped spring provides constant fresh water.

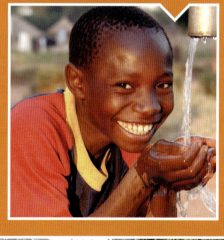

Top 10 Water Facts

Most rainy days	Mount Waialeale, Hawaii, has up to 350 rainy days per year.	
Fewest rainy days	In Arica, Chile, it rains about one day every six years.	
Most rain in 1 day	At Cilaos, La Réunion, it rained over 73 inches in one day.	
Tallest dam	The Rogun Dam in Tajikistan is 984 feet high.	
Biggest iceberg	Before the Antarctic B15 iceberg broke into pieces, it was over 4,200 square miles. That is larger than Jamaica.	
Longest river	The Nile is 4,132 miles long, running through Tanzania, Uganda, Sudan, and Egypt.	
Highest waterfall	Angel Falls in Venezuela is 3,212 feet high.	
Deepest ocean	The Mariana Trench in the Pacific Ocean is almost 7 miles deep.	
Deepest lake	Lake Baikal in Russia is 5,371 feet deep.	
Worst flood	The Huang He River flooded in China in 1931, killing 3,700,000 people.	

Glossary

accessible (uhk SEHS uh buhl) easy to get

acid rain (A sihd rayn) rain that contains harmful chemicals

agriculture (AG rih cuhl tyur) farming

brackish (BRAK ihsh) slightly salty

condensation (kahn duhn SAY shuhn) the process of changing from a gas to a liquid

dams (dams) barriers that hold back water

dense (dehns) crowded; compact

desalination (dee sah lih NA shuhn) the process of removing the salt from salt water, leaving drinkable fresh water

ecosystems (EE koh sihs tuhm) communities of species interacting with each other and their environments

evaporation (ee va por AY shuhn) the process of liquid becoming a vapor

fertilizers (FUHR tuh LY zuhrz) chemicals that make plants grow faster

generate (JEHN uhr ayt) to create

glaciers (GLAY shuhr) slow-moving bodies of ice made by the buildup of snow

hydroelectric (HY droh ee LEK trihk) creating electricity from falling water

ice caps (IHS kap) masses of ice that permanently cover a large area of land

ice sheet (IHS sheet) very large ice caps; the only ice sheets are currently in Greenland and Antarctica

impurities (ihm PYUR uh teez) particles that keep water from being clean

industry (IHN duhz tree) a large-scale business or group of businesses

infiltration (ihn fihl TRAY shuhn) the slow movement of water from the Earth's surface down through open spaces in the ground

irrigating (IHR ih gay teeng) watering land in order to grow crops

massive (MAS ihv) big and heavy

microscopic (my krow SKAH pihk) too small to be seen by the human eye

pesticides (PEHS tuh syds) chemicals used to kill pests, such as insects and rodents

polluted (puh LOO tuhd) made unclean; contaminated

pollutant (puh LOO tuhnt) waste that contaminates water, air, or soil

precipitation (pree sihp uh TAY shuhn) any form of water that falls from clouds: rain, snow, hail, sleet, or mist

purified (PYUR uh fyd) made clean

reservoirs (REH sur vwars) places where water is collected and used

sanitation (sah nuh TAY shuhn) the way that water and waste is handled to protect people's health

scarce (skayrs) hard to find; rare

sewage (SOO uhj) human waste

source (sohrs) the beginning of a brook or river; spring; fountain

water mains (WAH tuhr maynz) a system of water pipes

wetland (WEHT luhnd) swamps and marshes

Index